for my father

*and for my essential companions:
my wife, Susan,
and our sons, Evan and Whitman*

It appears to me natural that you should tell me, as a companion, what you decide, in order that I may not be caught unprepared, for I also have to travel.

—Father Pablo Font to Juan Bautista de Anza, while visiting California in 1776

Without companions, the world is a sea of stories with no one to listen.

—Kelsey Parker, freshman, Burlingame High School

PRAISE for *The English Teacher's Companion*

If ever a book deserved to be called *The English Teacher's Companion*, this is that book. This book is absolutely crammed with truly helpful advice and practical ideas for teaching, backed up by anecdotes of actual experiences galore. I believe that there is nobody, at any level of English teaching, who cannot benefit from this book. Here is advice for teaching literature, advice for teaching writing, advice for teaching thinking. Here is very sound thinking about the curriculum, about assessment, and about such new directions as media and computer literacy. Here, as Dryden said of Chaucer, is God's plenty. All of us who teach English can learn from this book and should have it on our shelves as a ready reference.

—**Robert Scholes**, Andrew W. Mellon Professor of Humanities, Brown University
Author of *The Rise and Fall of English*

Jim Burke's *The English Teacher's Companion* represents the hard-earned professional wisdom of an experienced and expert classroom practitioner—a teacher who has also made it his business to become impressively well informed on the best ideas and theories about teaching that are to be found in our professional literature. It's difficult to imagine a serious question about the teaching of English in the secondary classroom that Jim Burke doesn't address in his encyclopedic volume. And the answers he provides to those questions are unfailingly informed by a deep understanding of contemporary students, of the culture of the contemporary high school, of the political and social contexts in which teachers work, and of the best practices known to our professional community.

This book will serve as its title suggests, as the teaching companion for every new teacher and most experienced teachers of the current generation. It will be to the teaching of English in our time what Dr. Spock's *Baby Book* was to child care for my generation of parents.

—**Sheridan Blau**, President, National Council of Teachers of English

Want to know what to give the new English teacher? Or an old one? Jim Burke's book is it! Jim Burke has given us an inspiring view of secondary English teaching in which he weaves together educational politics (the standards movement, censorship), his reflections with a rich network of teaching friends (Bill Robinson, Pat Hanlon, Carol Jago), and the core of his classrooms—the subject and the students. Along the way, he gives us his love of teaching and his insights into teaching literature, grammar, composition, media studies. Yes, even how to organize the room and to enjoy parent night. Here is a chance to meet one of the very best.

—**Miles Myers**, Former Executive Director of the National Council of Teachers of English
Author of *Changing Our Minds: Negotiating English and Literacy*

Classroom instruction in the next century will be characterized by Burke's instructional approach, and teachers—both beginning and experienced—will benefit from the vision and insights revealed in this volume.

—**Jeffrey N. Golub**, University of South Florida
Author of *Activities for an Interactive Classroom*

When Jim's brother began teaching high school, a veteran master teacher named George took him under his wing. For those of us not fortunate enough to have a George in our life, there's Jim Burke's *The English Teacher's Companion*. In this book, Burke covers the theoretical from reading and writing theory to digital literacy and the practical from handling open house and parent-teacher conferences to teaching Shakespeare and vocabulary/grammatical conventions. Each chapter concludes with a thought for reflection, an activity to try, and a reading recommendation. The final section of the book is addressed to the new and preservice teacher, but every teacher will benefit from the discussion of politics and professionalism. Burke's book—filled with assignments, activities, stories from real classrooms, and down-to-earth planning advice—is the companion every teacher needs.

—**Kathleen and Jim Strickland**, Slippery Rock University
Authors of *Un-covering the Curriculum* and *Reflections on Assessment*